the heart of the
SPORTSMAN

strategies, tips, and thoughts for going beyond the chase

"*The Heart of the Sportsman* is a book every hunter will enjoy. I couldn't wait until the next story. I felt like I was there in the field with him. Jason's insights are gleaned from a world that I and countless others understand and love with a passion—the hunter's woods. You're gonna like this book!"

Steve Chapman, Recording Artist and Author
A Look at Life from a Deer Stand, What a Hunter Brings Home

"Jason will show you how to be a better hunter and fisherman. But more importantly, his insights into God's creation and his love for Christ can change your life forever. This book is a must for all sportsmen—young and old alike."

Charlie Alsheimer, Field Editor
Deer & Deer Hunting Magazine

"As you read these pages, you will open your mind to simple tactics that have proven themselves in the outdoors—and open your heart to words spoken softly and gently by God."

Charles Sorrells, President and Founder
Harvest Calls, Inc.

"Jason Cruise has found a way, with God's help, to interlock the hunter's mind with a wonderful, entertaining, and potentially life-changing message. What an awesome book!"

David Blanton, Executive Producer
Realtree Outdoors

"Jason Cruise is a seasoned guide that I would willingly follow on my adventures into God's Word."

Jimmy Sites, Producer and Host
Spiritual Outdoor Adventures

the heart of the
SPORTSMAN

strategies, tips, and thoughts for going beyond the chase

JASON CRUISE

BROADMAN
& HOLMAN
PUBLISHERS
Nashville, Tennessee

FOREVER INDEBTED

To the Lord Jesus . . .
for knowing me personally and yet loving me even still—
and for all that You've created in the outdoors.

To my wife, Michelle . . .
for your support (and tolerance) of my outdoor pursuits.
You're the best!

To Larry and Nancy Cruise . . .
for encouraging me to pursue my dreams.
You're the best parents a boy could have.

To all my family . . .
for your consistent love and undying support.

To the members of Belmont Heights . . .
for supporting me in my efforts to reach outdoorsmen for Christ.

*To David Hale, Steve Chapman, Charles Sorrells,
Charlie Alsheimer, Jimmy Sites, and David Blanton . . .*
for helping promote this project. You're a Christlike influence in the industry.

To landowners across the nation . . .
for the privilege of letting me pursue my passion for the outdoors.

Broadman & Holman Publishers
Nashville, Tennessee
broadmanholman.com

ISBN 0-8054-3094-6

All Scriptures are taken from the
HOLMAN CHRISTIAN STANDARD VERSION®
Copyright © 1999, 2000, 2002, 2004
by Holman Bible Publishers

Photographs on pages 20, 21, 23, 63, 67, 69, 70, 85
courtesy of SuperflaugeGAME® by Lynch*

Dewey Decimal Classification 242.64
Devotional Literature / Hunting / Nature

Printed in Mexico
1 2 3 4 07 06 05 04

SCOUTING REPORT

FOREWORD

What a brilliant way of taking hunting experiences and using them to teach us how to live a spiritual life. Jason has put together a masterpiece consisting of tips, techniques, and experiences which emphasize that winning and losing are not important, but how we play that game.

Our lives are the same way. For those of us who know Christ, it is easy to see where Jason is coming from. But for those of us who love to hunt but seldom stop to see God's handiwork, be careful reading this book, because you just might wind up accepting Christ as your Savior and gain eternal life in heaven. I am sure glad I did that already.

As you read this book, you will realize that the questions about how to harvest this animal or that animal, whether to let this one live or that one live, may seem important. But the real question is: will it be heaven or hell? Thank you, Jason, for helping answer this question.

This book was written for any sportsman who is seeking knowledge, wisdom, or success. That is just about everyone, is it not?

David Hale
Co-founder, Knight & Hale Game Calls

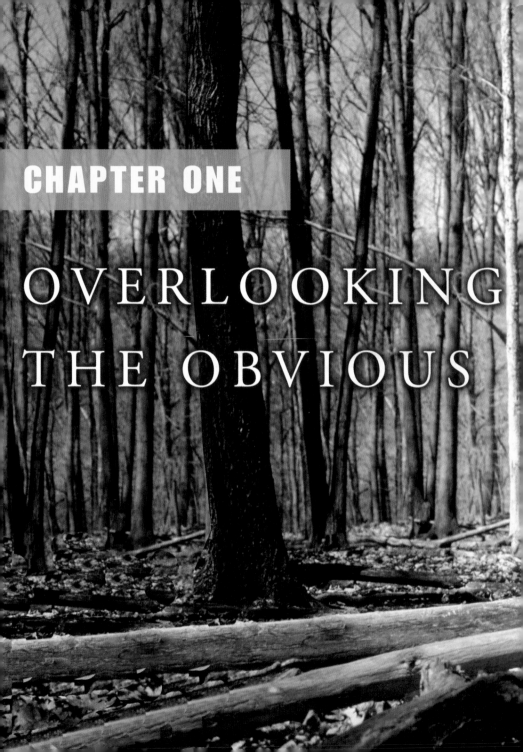

CHAPTER ONE

OVERLOOKING THE OBVIOUS

amouflage has come a long way since I started hunting. Back then, as you know, we all wore the standard "government issue"—army green and black. This was basically the hunter's staple, and at the time it was pretty much the only pattern to choose from.

But not so today!

I'm fascinated at the precision of the different patterns we now have access to, and I can't stress enough how important it is to have different patterns for different seasons.

- I use an early fall pattern for September.
- I don a different pattern for October and November.
- And I even change again for the dead of winter season.

The same goes for turkey hunting. As the environment "greens up," so does my camo. I want every advantage I can get to fool that ol' Tom.

TURKEY DAY PARADE

The advantage of a good camo pattern really came home to me during a turkey hunt not too long ago. It was one of those picture perfect April mornings. Norman Rockwell couldn't have painted a better landscape! The air was crisp and fresh, the sky cloudless, and the woods literally alive with spring.

I was loafing down a logging road around noon—actually on my way to the truck to pack it in for the day—when I saw some movement. I eased up to a field only to see several turkeys about five hundred yards from me, crossing a deep valley that split the field.

Here we go! The game is on!

I set up on the field edge in the shadows, got my strikers and calls strategically laid out beside me, and began to communicate. First a few clucks. Then a series of cutts. Even on a day as windy as this one, I felt sure they could hear me—even though they continued on their course away from me.

But as I began to call more aggressively, one bird turned my way . . . and gobbled. I knew if he would commit, the others most likely would, too.

They did.

One by one, they started walking my way. As the birds came within shooting range, I could see that the most mature bird of the six was a young tom with a beard of about seven inches.

I decided to pass.

AS I BEGAN TO CALL MORE AGGRESSIVELY, ONE BIRD TURNED MY WAY . . . AND GOBBLED.

I chose instead just to watch these birds for a while, up close and personal. As I hunkered there by an old oak, every one of the young strutters inched within twenty yards of me. Pinned down! I was afraid even to blink! One of the birds even came within eight steps of me, looking hard for that hen he *knew* he'd heard!

I sat there amazed that animals with their kind of eyesight—far keener than 20/10 vision—could be so close to me, yet have no idea I was there. I was *right in front of their eyes*, yet they were clueless to my presence.

Or is it really so amazing after all?

Am I perhaps just as guilty of overlooking the obvious?

LOOKING BUT NOT SEEING

I grew up in the outdoor world. My daddy owned and operated a small outdoor store in southeast Tennessee, a little place appropriately called "The Sportsman." Though small, it was a super cool place to grow up. We sold hunting and fishing gear, had a little deli for sandwiches, and—more than anything—it provided an outdoor-rich environment for friends and travelers.

It was a neat hangout.

Growing up in that kind of setting provided me the opportunity to go afield with some unique characters in the outdoor world. I learned how to successfully hunt and fish at an accelerated pace . . . just by being around those guys. The outdoors became an obsession for me, right from the start.

I WAS RIGHT IN FRONT OF THEIR EYES, YET THEY WERE CLUELESS TO MY PRESENCE.

That's why from the youngest age, I wanted to be good at hunting and fishing. The problem with that approach, though, is that—yes, you can end up with a lot of trophies on your wall—but you can also wind up missing some of the most important aspects of the outdoors.

For example, I spent season after season traversing all over God's creation yet overlooking His signature, not realizing the truth of that verse in the Bible that tells us: when God created the earth and all that is within it, He gave us signs which point to His reality.

The first chapter of Romans, verse 20, tells us that God's eternal power and presence are revealed in His creation, in the outdoors. Not *concealed,* but *revealed!* This power-packed verse of Scripture proves that even if God had never sent Jesus to make it perfectly clear, He had already pointed us to the fact that He exists *just by creating the earth.* With as many hours as I spent in the outdoors, God left me with no excuses to deny His presence. Through creation alone He had left me *millions* of clues!

The turkeys, see, had an excuse for not noticing me. I was clad in the best gear the camo industry has to offer. I was doing my dead-level best to remain concealed from my quarry.

But God had deliberately left many clues for me. He had done His best to be revealed before me through His incredible creation.

THE HAND OF GOD

So that spring morning when the young toms got so close to me, looking but not seeing with those incredible little black eyes of theirs, I realized we held some similarities.

Just look at what's right in front of *our* eyes.

• The next time you get outdoors, don't miss that sunrise. It was painted for you by the Eternal Artist whose palette never runs dry. Sunrise over a lake is not beautiful by accident.

• Don't overlook the colors of the field as the sun hits them for the first time since yesterday's nightfall.

- When you hear that heart-jolting gobble, remember it was His plan to give such a distinct sound to that critter.

- And what about the smell of the woods in the fall? That aroma was His idea.

Those sights, sounds, and fragrances are no mistake. They are there for a reason. They were created by the great hand of a loving God. They were placed there so that you and I would not overlook the obvious.

From the creation of the world His invisible attributes, that is, His eternal power and divine nature, have been clearly seen, being understood through what He has made. As a result, people are without excuse.

—Romans 1:20

CAMO TIPS THAT WORK

REMEMBER THE GOLDEN RULE OF CAMO

No camo will effectively hide movement. Yes, with today's amazing patterns you can get away with a little more movement than you used to. Do understand, however, that an animal will spot your movement long before he spots you just sitting there.

WATCH YOUR BACK

Hunters often put up stands or blinds that only have structure in *front* of them. But if I'm forced to choose, I want something *behind* me – especially in a tree stand. Always be aware of your profile and silhouette. What's behind you is more important than what's in front of you.

USE THE EXISTING TOOLS GOD GIVES YOU

Don't overlook fallen-down trees, or the stealth of setting up in the shade, or the subtle contours in the land and any other all-natural elements. When you learn to look for them, you'll be amazed how many tools are already out there in the woods with you.

CHOOSE PATTERNS THAT ARE LOCATION SPECIFIC

This is an important feature that's often overlooked. If you're turkey hunting, for example, a pattern that resembles the forest floor is key. If you're in a tree stand, however, forest floor patterns are not the best choice. In that case you want a pattern that's open and airy. Believe it or not, some bow hunters even use a snow and branch pattern in September! Because when a deer looks up, he doesn't see logs and stumps. He sees branches, leaves . . . and sky!

CHOOSE PATTERNS THAT ARE SEASON SPECIFIC

With today's variety of camo, there's really no excuse for mistakes here. You should change your camo as the seasons change. When turkey hunting, your camo needs to "green up" to match the coming of spring as it gets later in the season. When deer hunting, let your camo "die out" as the foliage gets more brown and dry.

MAKING A FASHION STATEMENT IS <u>NOT</u> THE HUNTER'S GOAL

Here's where a lot of hunters really mess up. Don't wear the same camo pattern on both your upper and lower body. You honestly will look too good! The goal is to break up your outline. For instance, I'll use forest floor patterns when hunting on the ground. In a tree, though, I'll wear two different patterns that both have open, airy designs. Remember . . . the woods are broken up with shades, contour, and color – and you should be, too!

CHAPTER TWO

HUNTING
FOR ALL
THE
WRONG
REASONS

November is a super month to deer hunt. The whitetail's hormones are changing weekly, and the hunting action changes with it, proving to be my favorite time of the year to be in the woods. But it was at this time of year—hunting in early November a few years back—when I experienced a tough challenge to my hunting ego.

The farm I was hunting had open fields which I had to negotiate before reaching my stand. I hunted my way to my setup in the peeking sunrise light, as I usually do in such a situation. (I've found I tend to bump more deer when crossing a field edge in the dark. So years ago I began to wait until light to start my trek. It's proven to be a very successful tactic. This hunt proved no different!)

I HUNTED MY WAY TO MY SETUP IN THE PEEKING SUNRISE LIGHT.

Easing my way quickly and quietly down a wood line along a field's edge, I saw two slick heads come over a rise in the field. Behind them was ol' Mossy Horns. The does' scent was hot, and he was in full pursuit—like Barney Fife on steroids. And I could not get him to stop.

Finally, after blaring something close to a scream into my grunt tube, I got him to halt for just a quick second.

I shot.

He bolted into the woods.

The shot felt good. I gave it a few minutes, reloaded my Knight rifle, and then moved up cautiously to the tree line where he entered the woods.

No blood.

But that was no big deal, because we've all bagged bucks that didn't bleed much but were down not far from where we shot them.

This time, however, I found no blood at all. After looking vigorously for two hours, I finally concluded that I had simply missed that big buck.

FAILURE AT ITS FINEST

To be quite candid with you, I was "emotionally disturbed." I don't think I've ever been as angry with myself in a hunting situation. I was losing my perspective of why I hunt in the first place. But I just couldn't help it. There was a brewing storm in my bones which I simply could not shake.

I was losing my perspective of why I hunt in the first place.

I sat down under a white oak in the middle of the woods and felt sorry for myself. You don't have to say it, because I know: it was a stupid, immature reaction from a veteran hunter who's taken his share of bucks. I should have been happy with my hunting life, but at that moment I was certainly not happy. I was so disgusted, in fact, that I packed it in, not just for the day, but for the entire trip! I had taken five days off, and this was just the second day. But I was so beside myself that I got in my truck and drove two hours to get back home.

Bummed.

SECOND CHANCE

A few days later, a hunting buddy of mine talked me into heading to one of his farms. I went, although I was still chewing myself out for that missed opportunity.

I got on stand before daylight and was just sitting there—with very little hunting gusto—when I heard the familiar steps of a deer approaching. In the dim light of that fall morning, I saw a nice buck—even bigger than the buck I had missed seventy-two hours before! He was walking behind and away from me at an angle.

After an intense chess match of calling to him with various grunt sequences, I got him to change directions and commit my way. I shot him at a hundred yards.

This time it was no miss!

I got down from my tree and noticed that his rack seemed to get bigger with every step I took! He was a heavy nine-pointer that dressed out at 174 pounds.

John Denver's words came home to me: "Some days are diamonds, some days are stones." Tuesday had been a rock hard day, but Friday was a perfect carat! As I drove to the checking station with that prized buck in the back of my truck, it hit me: if I had connected with that deer on Tuesday, I'd have never hunted again on Friday.

Man, was I ever thankful for missing that Tuesday buck!

SOME DAYS ARE DIAMONDS,
SOME DAYS ARE STONES.

We know that all things work together for the good of those who love God; those who are called according to His purpose.

—Romans 8:28

WINNING AND LOSING

It's true that life is no cakewalk. We experience a lot of defeats—sometimes way too many. Failure is simply a part of life. I mean, show me someone who's never experienced failure, and I'll show you someone who's never really pushed themselves to the edge. Armchair quarterbacks are wonderful athletes until they actually have to get in the game. They think they know everything, and they think they've never lost, at least not in the stat column of their own fantasy driven mind!

SHOW ME SOMEONE WHO'S NEVER EXPERIENCED FAILURE, AND I'LL SHOW YOU SOMEONE WHO'S NEVER REALLY PUSHED THEMSELVES TO THE EDGE.

Yet we so easily fall into this trap, thinking failure should never happen. True failure, though, means to quit and never try again. Sometimes we lose—we attempt something and it just doesn't succeed. But there's a big difference between losing and failure. It's bad to lose; it's tragic to fail.

That November morning, however, I failed—not because I missed a large buck, but because I quit when things got tough.

Often in life, we get handed cards which seem impossible to play out. And what do we do? We seek out lonely white oaks to sit under and complain. One single "stone" experience can blind us to the fact that God is always working for our good, turning stones into diamonds.

If you don't believe me, then just check out Romans 8:28: "We know that in all things God works for the good of those who love him, who have been called according to his purpose."

Though God never promised us smooth sailing, He did promise us continual support, unlimited resources, and sustaining power which cannot be found through any other source. I'm talking about real power. Power to overcome and continue. Power that no humanistic self-help conference can give you. Power that gives you an endless supply of depth in your life.

So hang on, because a diamond day could be coming around sooner than you think.

I pray that the eyes of your heart may be enlightened so you may know what is the hope of His calling, what are the glorious riches of His inheritance among the saints, and what is the immeasurable greatness of His power to us who believe.   —Ephesians 1:18-19

"It is not the critic who counts, not the man who points out how the strong man stumbled or where the doer of deeds could have done better. The credit belongs to the man who is actually in the arena; whose face is marred by dust and sweat and blood; who strives valiantly; who errs and comes short again and again; who knows the great enthusiasms, the great devotion, and spends himself in a worthy cause; who, at the best, knows in the end the triumph of high achievement; and who, at the worst, if he fails, at least fails while daring greatly, so that his place shall never be with those cold and timid souls who know neither victory nor defeat."

—Theodore Roosevelt

CHAPTER THREE

LISTENING TO THE WRONG VOICES

I t was a cold, clear November morning. You know the type. The frosty fall air had a bite to it, and the ground was brittle. It was one of those mornings when you can't help but make noise as you walk. You feel like each step you take over the white-capped forest floor is equivalent to shouting, *"Hey, buck, here I come!"*

But it was a neat day for me. I was just fifteen years old and about to try deer calling for the very first time in my life. And within ten minutes of clashing the antlers, I had already rattled one up.

Here's how it happened: I positioned myself on the ground in an area where I knew the deer frequented, and I decided to give it a try. After a few sequences of clashing the antlers together, I just sat still . . . waiting. Ten minutes later—no kidding—I heard steps approaching . . . quickly! Pretty soon I could see him, sweeping his head from side to side as he walked, looking intently for the battling bucks that were invading his territory. Squeezing the trigger, I initiated myself into the world of calling whitetails.

WHITETAILS, THE MOST ELUSIVE AND SILENT CREATURES I KNOW, DO IN FACT "TALK"

Dragging a deer out of the woods that day changed my deer hunting mind-set forever, and made me a firm believer that whitetails, the most elusive and silent creatures I know, do in fact "talk"—you just have to know their language.

CALL OF THE WILD

I love to use deer calls when I hunt. They simply boost my odds of bagging a buck. Even on slow mornings, calling makes me feel like I'm at least doing something to turn the game in my favor. I firmly believe that most hunters don't call simply because they don't know the power of vocalizations. Most hunters are slow to believe that whitetails are vocal animals.

Even though I've been calling for years now, it wasn't too long ago when I called in my biggest buck to date. He was a large, mature, four-year-old brute. It was the week of the first black powder season in my state—a time when mature bucks are often killed, because this week usually finds a strong pre-rut in full swing. I'll bet my bank account on the fact that the buck I shot that day would still be in the woods were it not for my calling to him.

Let's study this hunt . . .

He came from behind me right at daylight. If he'd come through two minutes earlier, I'd have probably been in trouble—it was that early! He came from behind my left shoulder, entered a small clearing, then threw his head up to scope for a potential mate. No girls were around, though, so he quickly moved away from me at a good canter: nose dipping low, nose swinging high, trying to pick up a scent.

I grunted.

He stopped.

I let out a few more grunts, each with a slightly different pitch. He turned my way, but didn't move.

After a few seconds, he started moving away from me at the same quick

HE SLAPPED
A TREE
WITH HIS
RACK!

pace, trolling the woods, looking for a girlfriend. I changed grunt calls quickly, then began to pick up the intensity with some different vocalizations. I mixed up my tones in both pitch and length. In a flash he turned 180 degrees and came right at me. Then when he got within a hundred yards, he did something I've yet to see a buck do—before or since. He slapped a tree with his rack! I'm not talking about simply head-butting a tree and rubbing it furiously; I'm talking about slapping a tree like a boxer in a knock-down, drag-out fight!

During that moment, I aided him in "giving up the ghost."

VOICES IN THE DARK

When you really think about it in its simplest form, I fooled that big buck. To me, calling whitetails is the ultimate game of deception. That buck heard voices which sounded somewhat authentic, but in reality they were an empty promise. He hangs on my wall today because he listened to the wrong voices.

Life is full of communication. Advertisements and marketing schemes throw messages at us all day long. Internet ads explode in our faces, daring us to try a new technique that will only lead to more debt or even moral failure. In today's world, finding a filter for the heart is a basic survival technique, because communication is all around us. Some of it is sound advice; some is advice that's just full of sound. Yet we're often tempted to follow the wrong voices because our motives are misplaced. We think we can get away with it, yet we fail to realize that what sounds authentic is sometimes nothing more than an imposter waiting to do us in.

Right now in your life . . . who are you listening to?

Instead of having your heart and emotions driven like a leaf in the wind, why not choose stability? Isn't that the best choice? One thing's for sure: with God you can be sure that you'll never be misled!

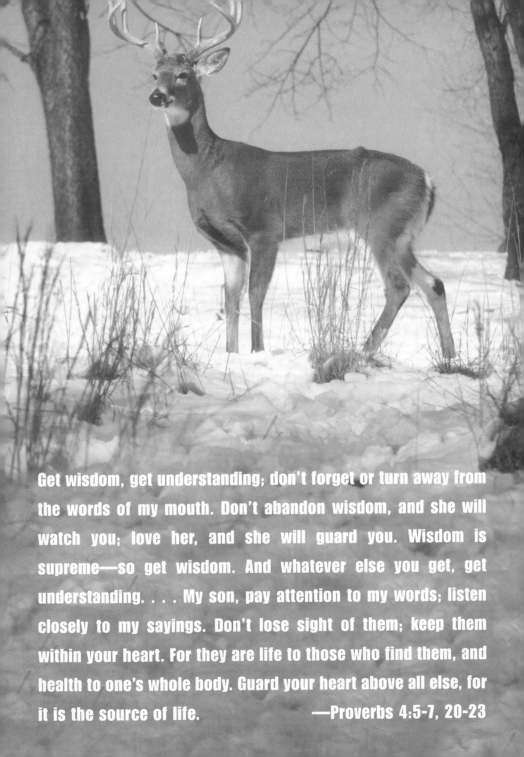

Get wisdom, get understanding; don't forget or turn away from the words of my mouth. Don't abandon wisdom, and she will watch you; love her, and she will guard you. Wisdom is supreme—so get wisdom. And whatever else you get, get understanding. . . . My son, pay attention to my words; listen closely to my sayings. Don't lose sight of them; keep them within your heart. For they are life to those who find them, and health to one's whole body. Guard your heart above all else, for it is the source of life.

—Proverbs 4:5-7, 20-23

SEVEN TRUTHS TO MAKE CALLING WORK FOR YOU

IF YOU DON'T CALL, YOU HAVE A 100% CHANCE OF NOT SEEING A DEER

The grand lie many hunters buy into is that they don't believe calling works. I know for a fact it does, because I've experienced its benefits too many times. If you don't call, you are guaranteed to experience nothing!

BE COMPLETELY STILL AND READY TO SHOOT <u>BEFORE</u> YOU CALL

All I had to do when that deer came into range was pull the trigger. A deer's always looking hard for any movement, and if he sees you move, you're most likely busted!

PREDETERMINE WHAT KIND OF SOUNDS YOU WANT TO VOCALIZE

I plan ahead of time what calls I want to vocalize before I begin calling. This reduces error, and it gives me a game plan. With this particular buck, I started with non-abrasive, social/contact grunts. When that didn't work, I moved to more aggressive grunt vocalizations.

NEVER MAKE THE SAME SOUND TWICE

Many hunters are willing to experiment with a grunt call, but the sound comes out so bland, the call's not attractive. An average caller will simply let out an "urp-urp-urp." But think about it: do you enjoy conversations with people who have boring, monotone voices? Your calling pitch — especially when grunting aggressively — needs to resemble voice inflections or movement in pitch.

USE MORE THAN ONE TYPE OF GRUNT CALL

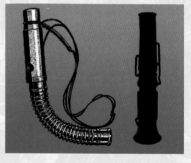

We can take a lesson from duck hunters; they carry all kinds of calls to the blind. Turkey hunters wouldn't dream of carrying only a slate call in their vest. So would somebody please tell me why most deer hunters carry only one grunt call into the woods? Remember the buck I shot? My first set of calls piqued his attention, but he didn't engage. He didn't submit to my calling until I had changed to a different call which produced a different pitch.

DON'T OVERCALL, AND DON'T CALL TOO LOUD

Many hunters blast away at their grunts. It's true that a deer can't respond if he can't hear you, so you shouldn't be afraid to lay down loudly on a call. But usually a moderate amount of volume will suffice. Also, you don't want to continue calling forever if the deer doesn't respond. Don't *give up* easily, but don't scream at him if he doesn't respond.

IF A DEER ENGAGES YOUR CALLING, SHUT UP!

If he starts your way, don't make another sound unless he hangs up for a long time just out of range. When the buck I've been telling you about turned my way and began to move in, the only sound he heard from me was my muzzle blast! If a deer responds, most likely he's bought into the game and he'll come on into range. Continuing to call only increases the odds that you'll make a sound he doesn't like. Then you'll only drag your gun back to the truck!

DISPELLING THE MYTHS OF CALLING

MYTH #1: YOU ONLY NEED TO TRY CALLING WHEN THE RUT IS ON

Many hunters say deer calling only works when deer are more hormonal due to the pre-rut or when the rut is in full swing. If that were true, it would basically imply that whitetails only "talk" for about two weeks out of the year. Let me ask you: do you only talk to your fellow humans from late October to mid-November? Deer talk year-round; you just have to know when and how to call them during certain phases. Many hunters I know won't call during early archery season. I can promise you from personal experience – they are cheating themselves!

MYTH #2: ONLY CALL WHEN YOU SEE A DEER, BECAUSE COLD CALLING DOESN'T WORK

This is one hundred percent false! Cold calling (calling when you don't actually see a deer) works very well. In fact, I'd say eighty percent of the deer I call in are from cold calling. Just because I couldn't see them, that didn't mean they weren't within earshot of my current location.

MYTH #3: YOU MUST BE ABLE TO MAKE A WIDE VARIETY OF SOUNDS TO CALL WHITETAILS

It's true that you must be able to mix up your calling, but you don't need to make every sound a whitetail makes in order to call one in. There are a few bread-and-butter calls you need to master. I call them (1) the social or contact grunt, (2) the semi-aggressive grunt, and (3) the aggressive grunt.

MYTH #4: YOU MUST BE A CALLING EXPERT TO CALL IN DEER

You won't see me at game-calling contests, because I'm no pro. What I do have, though, is experience in the field. Don't think that calling only works for those game-calling champions you see on TV. You can make calling work for you!

CHAPTER FOUR

FISHING FRUSTRATION

HOW YOU HANDLE DIFFICULTY
OFTEN DETERMINES THE OUTCOME

Have you ever been fishing one of your favorite holes only to find that after you've been there a good, long while, nothing is happening?

Same lure or fly, same time of day, similar conditions to days when you've caught fish there before. Still, it seems the fish have a certifiable case of lockjaw, and there's not a thing you can do about it.

What is your first gut reaction? Cut your losses and move on, right? Most of the time that's exactly what we do. And truth be told, moving is sometimes our best option.

But patience is often what wins the day.

MY DAD, THE BASSMASTER

My dad knows smallmouth bass better than most people on the lake. I know that sounds biased, and it is! However, my bias doesn't necessarily come from being his son as much as from watching him routinely drag smallmouth out of the lake when everyone else—including me—were dragging nothing but our egos back to the boat.

One of the golden rules I learned as a kid from sitting under his teaching was this: Be patient and don't quit. The fish are usually there; it's just a matter of time, some extra thinking, and a little creativity before your work will pay off.

> **Be patient and don't quit. The fish are usually there, it's just a matter of time, some extra thinking, and a little creativity before your work will pay off.**

My dad's understanding of the smallmouth's underwater world did not pass down into my genetic code—which most likely explains why I turned to fly-fishing for trout. One thing's for sure, though: I still apply Dad's wisdom to my trout streams.

Trout, you know, are creatures of habit. They don't want to work hard for food if they don't have to. And they favor certain conditions over others. Once you find a hole that the trout call home, you can usually count on it producing fish for you pretty much anytime you venture out into the waters—maybe not always, but more often than not. They are there. So it's almost always a mistake to just give up when the fishing gets tough.

THE QUITTER IN US

The same can be said about life. You just can't let frustrating conditions get the best of you. Quitters never win and winners never quit . . . especially when you know that what you're doing has proven to be right in the past.

YOU JUST CAN'T LET FRUSTRATING CONDITIONS GET THE BEST OF YOU. QUITTERS NEVER WIN AND WINNERS NEVER QUIT, ESPECIALLY WHEN YOU KNOW THAT WHAT YOU'RE DOING HAS PROVEN TO BE RIGHT IN THE PAST.

If you only give your best effort for a short amount of time before giving up, then what lessons will you learn? If you quit too soon, how can your character be forged from the trials of life? Success is super sweet when it comes just moments before you think it's time to admit defeat.

Have you ever wondered why life is so often compared to storms? You can listen to just about any genre of music, and you'll eventually run across a song comparing life to storms. Perhaps the reason why life is many times compared to storms is simply because storms never stick around. They may linger, but they're not permanent. They roll in, only to pass.

God never promised us an easy life, but He did promise to be there every moment of every day, providing us with the answers on what to do next. Sometimes those answers seem to take a little longer to find, but just like your favorite fishing hole, He'll always produce!

SUCCESS IS SUPER SWEET WHEN IT COMES JUST MOMENTS BEFORE YOU THINK IT'S TIME TO ADMIT DEFEAT.

One thing I do: forgetting what is behind and reaching forward to what is ahead, I pursue as my goal the prize promised by God's heavenly call in Christ Jesus.

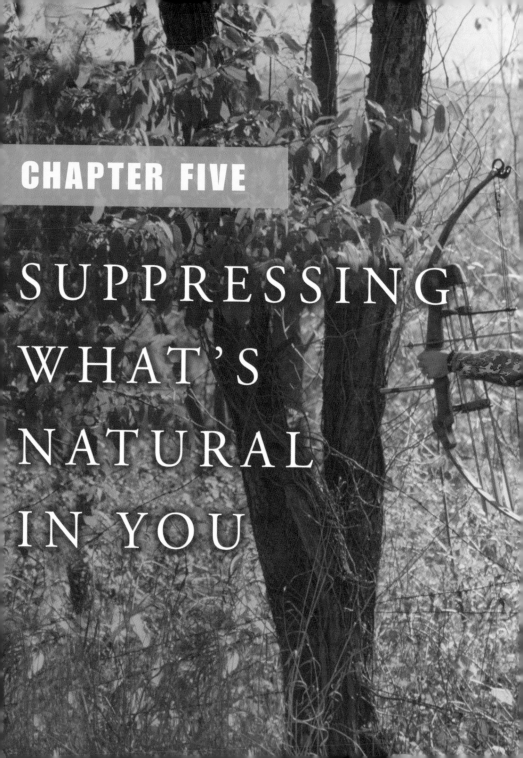

CHAPTER FIVE

SUPPRESSING WHAT'S NATURAL IN YOU

It's been said—and even proven through research—that to the white-tail's nose, humans absolutely stink! In fact, the research indicates that we don't just have a little "B.O." No, the news is worse than that, my friends. To the whitetail's nose, we are flat out *rank* when it comes to the stench we emit in the woods.

When I started hunting as a kid, the concepts and ideas which most of us held about scent control were quite vague. We all knew deer could smell us, but we didn't really know just how to eliminate our odor like we do today. Back then there were no scent containment suits, no odor-stopping deodorants and powders, and no soaps to make you as bacterially clean as most surgeons!

On top of that, technology was lagging behind in the area of deer scents. You could buy Doe-in-Heat, but pretty much everyone in my hunting circles was wary of it. We just didn't have the education we do now.

So we just did what we knew best . . . sprayed our boots in Red Fox Urine and tried to keep the wind to our favor.

Obviously, we owe a lot to today's technology. The carbon activated scent suppressant suits are unbelievably beneficial. The deodorants, powders, and soaps really do help with removing odor-causing bacteria from the hunter's body. And the variety of scents we have, along with the knowledge to back them up, seriously ups our odds of bagging a nice buck.

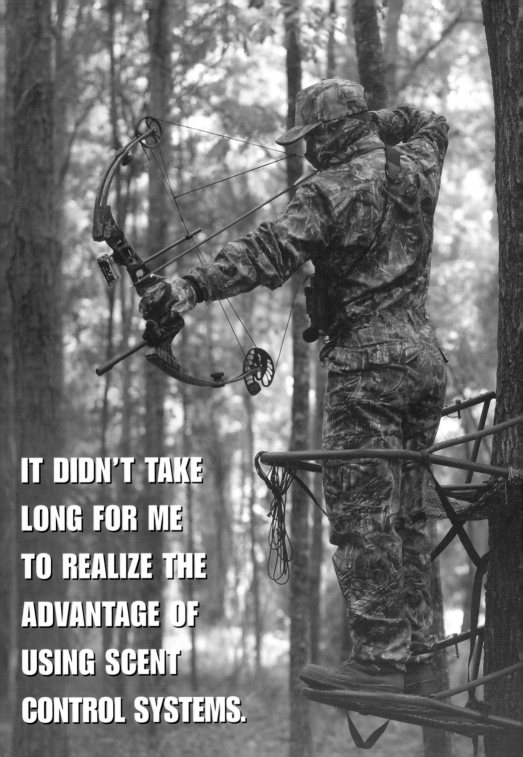

IT DIDN'T TAKE
LONG FOR ME
TO REALIZE THE
ADVANTAGE OF
USING SCENT
CONTROL SYSTEMS.

WHY IT'S SO STUPID TO STINK

It didn't take long for me to realize the advantage of using scent control systems. I've always been a hunter who'll do anything to get the edge on a whitetail, so when scent suppressant aids came out, I was more than willing to use them.

And I noticed an immediate change, especially in archery season.

In the South, where I live, archery season presents you with warm temperatures. It's not uncommon to have September evenings where you're battling temperatures of eighty degrees coupled with eighty-five percent humidity! When I started using scent suppressants, though, I noticed deer would get closer than normal, hang out longer, and feed off without knowing I was there. What a relief—when you consider that we were all getting pretty sick of having everything from yearlings to mature deer detect our presence from eighty yards away!

Yet even though we now have this gold mine of assets in high quality suppressants, I still know plenty of hunters who don't even use them. (Amazing!) How could any hunter justify deliberately reducing the odds of success?

Can you kill a nice buck without doing these things? Sure. But you won't do it consistently!

That's why I'm so obsessive about it!

Perhaps I cross the line into being obsessive/compulsive on this subject. I'll be the first to admit that I'm quirky when it comes to scent control. But I know that much of successful hunting comes down to doing the little things right. Believe it or not, some of the things I'll share with you later in the Strategy Session don't take a whole lot of extra effort—especially when you get used to them. But in that one great moment when you're standing over your buck, you realize that all your extra effort was worth it.

THE SCENT YOU SHOULDN'T SUPPRESS

To reject God is to first suppress Him from within, not from without.

The truth of the matter is: you can never fully suppress your scent. It's one of the most natural things about you. Odor is who you are. You can try, but you can only be successful up to a point . . . which brings me to another point:

To reject God is to first suppress Him from within, not from without.

FOR TO GOD WE ARE THE FRAGRANCE OF CHRIST.
—2 CORINTHIANS 2:15

We are made in His image; therefore, that longing in our hearts for something spiritual comes from Him. Before we can reject Him, first we have to suppress Him.

The Bible says that God has "set eternity in the hearts of men" (Ecclesiastes 3:11). If there were no such thing as God, then believe me, you would never have even contemplated your first spiritual thought. If we were just hollow, robotic people, then we would live absent of anything remotely spiritual.

The truth is, though, that every one of us has a part of our souls that is drawn to the spiritual. Why? Because we were created that way. There is a driving Force in the world—God—who causes us to seek after Him.

So fight your scent, but don't fight God! Suppress your scent, but don't suppress the God who made you!

It will make both the outdoors and all of life so much sweeter than you ever imagined.

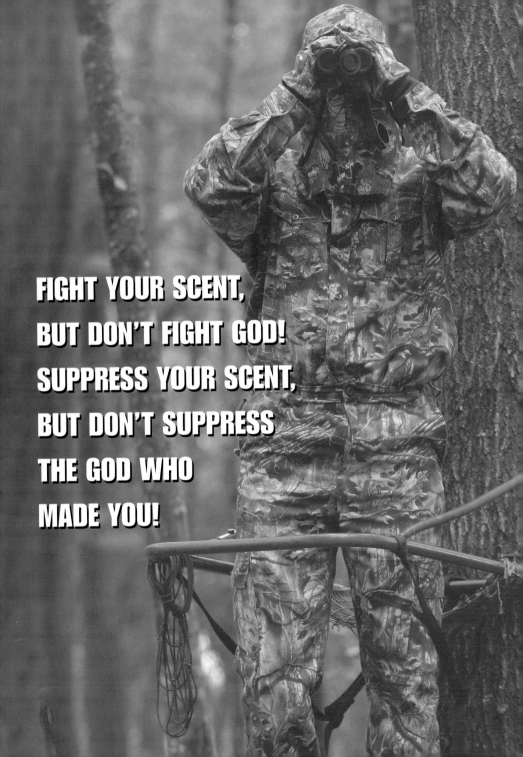

FIGHT YOUR SCENT,
BUT DON'T FIGHT GOD!
SUPPRESS YOUR SCENT,
BUT DON'T SUPPRESS
THE GOD WHO
MADE YOU!

STENCH STOPPERS

TAKE A BATH USING SCENT-FREE SOAPS AND DEODORANTS

This is a no-brainer step number one, and it's the most vital. Put those bacteria reducing soaps to work for your advantage. Moreover, be sure to take a bath during the same time frame of your hunt. Don't take a bath the night before. Bacteria will come back and hurt you.

WASH YOUR HAIR

Some research indicates that your hair is the most odor producing area of your body. A simple application of suppressant shampoo will take care of that. Another very effective thing you can do here is to use scent reducing powder. It wicks sweat away before it has time to leave bacteria. Pour it on your hands and rub it through your hair.

WASH YOUR CLOTHES FREQUENTLY AND STORE THEM SAFELY

I keep all my hunting clothes in hard plastic bins. I've found that they keep out scent pretty well, and they are economical to boot.

CHANGE INTO YOUR HUNTING GEAR AFTER YOU GET TO YOUR LAND

Many hunters make a grand mistake here. They go through all the trouble of bathing and washing their clothes in suppressant detergent, and then climb into a vehicle that smells of fast food, oil from the floor mat, or the odor of the fruity refresher they keep in their truck to make it smell good! All of these odors are foreign to the deer. Never forget that! That's why on my drive to the woods, I wear

old khaki pants, old boots, and a T-shirt. I don't put on my camo pants until I arrive, and then I don't wear anything up top but a T-shirt while I'm going to my tree – even in cold temperatures. I know I'm going to get warm walking in, and I don't want to defeat all my hard work by putting on my full gear only to have it cause me to sweat! I carry a backpack with all my clothes in it, and when I get to my location, I change clothes completely.

AVOID CONVENIENCE STORES LIKE THE PLAGUE

If you must have breakfast, then grab a granola bar or a muffin from home (it's better for you anyway), because the minute you walk into a store, your clothes smell like a pack of cigarettes, and your boots pick up all the oil and gas of a million vehicles that come through there every day. Hunters go into these bacteria infested places, take all that funk with them into the woods, and then complain that they only saw squirrels!

SPRAY DOWN LIGHTLY AFTER YOU GET OUT OF YOUR VEHICLE, AND THEN HEAVILY WHEN YOU GET TO YOUR LOCATION

You're going to get hot while walking in, so dress lightly and spray down enough to suppress your odor. Since you've already taken a bath, this should be sufficient to help you remain undetected.

CHAPTER SIX

RELATIONSHIPS: THE ULTIMATE TROPHY

There are defining moments in every outdoorsman's life, each of which you remember with acute detail. They are eternally engraved into your soul.

Your first gun.

Your first hunt.

The first time you hooked a fish.

Your first kill.

Among my greatest memories of hunting are these: a .410 single shot, the opening day of whitetail season 1982, the half-rack three-pointer that may has well have been a 210 class Boone & Crockett!

Each of these experiences are moments I'll never forget. And there's a treasure chest full of other memories just like them. They are burned into my heart, not only because I was knighted on these occasions as a "hunter," but because these events also hold within them the people who have played a major role in the drama of my life.

Each of us is involved in our own drama in life. For hunters, much of it is played out in the coliseum of the outdoors. At some point in our lives, the outdoors caught our attention and changed us. More often than not, it consumed us. And most likely, it still does. Only hunters understand Mossy Oak when they say, "It's not a passion. It's an obsession."

Yet there is still more to the outdoors than the kill.

THERE IS STILL
MORE TO THE
OUTDOORS
THAN THE KILL.

DAD

My dad is forever the major player in my outdoor story. I was three years old when he took me on my first hunt . . . a bear hunt! Oh, I wanted to hunt bears! Yes, bears! At three years old, mind you. Big, snarly, mangle-toothed bears. So I packed my heavy weaponry (consisting of a plastic sword and a toy knife) and went off with my dad, ready to face the beast.

He knew, of course, that there wasn't a bear anywhere in Coffee County. He knew there wasn't a bear in any county that *touched* Coffee County. And he knew there wasn't a bear in any county that touched a county that touched *Coffee* County!

But that wasn't the point. My dad knew that little boys needed adventure and the courage that comes from such moments. He also knew that I'd grow up some day and would need courage on a much greater, deeper level.

My adventure that day was in trying to find the great bruin and run him through with my sword. My *dad's* adventure was in trying to capture a son's heart in a lifelong, trusting relationship.

I took no trophy grizzly that day, but my dad found his prize: the launch of a journey to establish a bond with his son that would never be broken.

I took no trophy grizzly that day, but my dad found his prize: the launch of a journey to establish a bond with his son that would never be broken.

SO I PACKED MY HEAVY WEAPONRY (CONSISTING OF A PLASTIC SWORD AND A TOY KNIFE) AND WENT OFF WITH MY DAD, READY TO FACE THE BEAST.

LOST AND FOUND

> **I longed for all the relationships I'd formed over the years through the outdoors.**

As my hunting matured, I became as obsessed with it as you probably did. To conquer something wild, to beat an animal at its own game on its own turf—what a rush! You know the feeling exactly!

As the years ebbed, however, the conquering spirit didn't seem so strong anymore. I was older and still traversing the wilderness, but often by myself. Dad couldn't stand the cold anymore. Yes, I had other hunting friends, and that was nice. But it wasn't the same.

Eventually I moved away to college, then further on to pursue work on my master's degree. Yet I missed hunting. I didn't miss the kill, really, but I longed for all the relationships I'd formed over the years through the outdoors.

Upon completing my studies, I reunited with the weapons of my younger years. The beat-up Marlin 30-30 which still bore the signs of many battles. The bow I had used as a teenager. Many days I had spent with those familiar friends. We were reunited at last.

It felt right.

Even still, it wasn't as sweet as being in the woods with the people I'd shared those experiences with. But one missing piece was linked when I finally talked Dad into chasing toms with me. (He won't admit it now, but I really think he's sneaking up quickly on a gobbler addiction!) Together now, we often play those sweet spring chess matches with our wary opponents.

But when I hunt with Dad now, I have a different heart—a heart that understands just how precious this relationship truly is. Why do I understand the deeper side of hunting? Because my dad did. He instilled it in me when I was only three . . . on our first "bear hunt." From that day forward I've been bonded with my father. We're friends. Confidants.

We are together.

There are other people in this drama, too—many friends made along the way. Endless stacks of stories piled high into cords of memories. I've harvested a lot of creatures, and I've had a lot of fun doing it. I have the pictures which testify to these successful hunts.

But nothing can take the place of the people who have been and *still are* involved along the way. *Their* faces are in my pictures, too.

DEEP IN THE WOODS

Perhaps you love to hunt and fish just because you love the challenge. But I want to challenge you to go deeper. If you only hunt or fish because you love conquering wild game, then friend, you have no idea what you're missing.

What about the sunrise? Do you realize it is God's hand that paints the morning sky?

What about time with your son or daughter in a duck blind or on the lake? Daddys that spend time with their sons or daughters in the outdoors usually find that their kids stay off the streets and out of trouble. Could there be any more worthy investment?

What about conversations with your buddy as you help each other with real-life decisions? Those are the things which take place in the field, and yet you'll remember those moments long after you've forgotten how many birds you took home that day or how many fish you dragged in.

God gave us a lot when He gave us the outdoors. But one of the best things He gave us are the people who share the outdoors with us and the memories those times provide.

Relationships, strengthened by time in God's creation, are truly one of His greatest gifts to us.

If you only hunt because you love conquering wild game, you have no idea what you're missing.

CHAPTER SEVEN

TRICKING THE TOM

SOMETIMES YOU JUST CAN'T WIN

I had gotten on a bird right out of the gate that morning. Just as the sun was rising, I could hear him yelling from far away. There was a good size canyon-like hollow between us, and I could tell there was a shelf which somewhat connected the two ridges to my left. So I headed that direction hoping to find his strut zone.

Sure enough, as I made my way along the rim, I could hear him gobbling and coming my way.

Atop that rim was an old logging road connecting the two ridges. I had found his kitchen! I rested my decoys on their stakes, found a good sized oak to provide backrest, and got ready.

Calls in hand and mouth . . . let the games begin!

Little did I know that a *game* was truly what I was going to experience that morning.

BAIT AND SWITCH

I don't know if I've ever been as frustrated with a tom as I was with this one. He'd get within seventy yards, holler his head off, I'd ease my safety off, then he'd hang up. I honestly think he got a

I honestly think he got a sore throat from all that gobbling!

sore throat from all that gobbling! I'm quite sure he had to clear his throat a few times to muster up enough air to gobble. He was firing down furiously.

He'd start to backtrack, gobbling the whole time. I felt like he was literally taunting me! For an hour I was pinned down.

If I dared to move, I knew he'd take off like an F-16 streaking across the deck of an aircraft carrier!

I'd go silent for long intervals, just raking leaves and purring. He'd gobble hard. But after a while, I could tell that wasn't working.

I'd get aggressive and imitate several hens. He'd gobble like a maniac, but stay just out of sight and out of range.

Was I exposed in the sunlight? I wondered. No, I was in a shaded area like I needed to be. *Was there enough cover around me?* Yep.

I'm telling you, everything was in place!

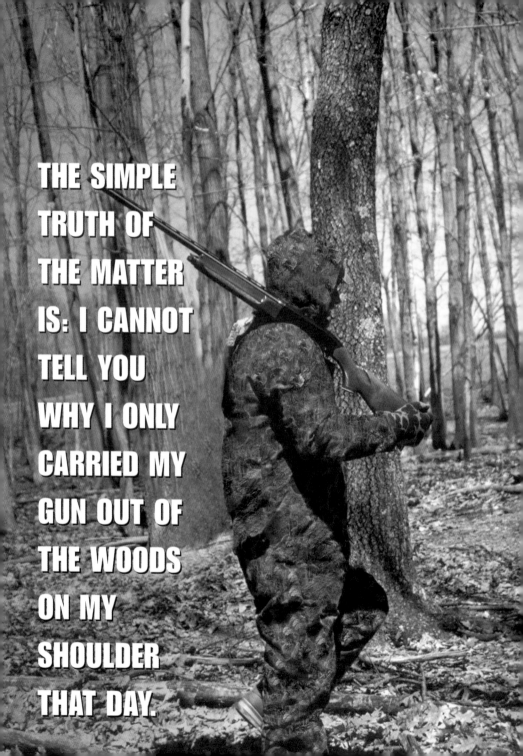

The simple truth of the matter is: I cannot tell you why I only carried my gun out of the woods on my shoulder that day. By all accounts, I did exactly what a turkey hunter should do in that situation.

OH, WELL

Sometimes our lives are a lot like that early April experience. There are things that happen to us which we simply cannot understand or even begin to explain. There's no reason for it. We do everything right, but somehow things just don't work out.

Even though turkey hunting—like much of life—is often out of our control, the good thing is that God is always in control. He never makes a mistake. He's always perfect.

Just knowing that fact sure does make life a lot easier for me. And it makes leaving the woods easier, too—because I know that my life doesn't revolve around whether or not I take that tom on that day.

My life just revolves around Him.

WORKING A WARY GOBBLER

DON'T GET IMPATIENT

You must know when to gamble and when to stay with the hand you're dealt. That's easy advice to give, but hard advice to follow. Do remember, however, that a turkey is on turkey time. He lives there. Getting in a hurry is not his usual response. Your best efforts at patience are minimal when compared to his patience level. So waiting him out is always my first move – or should I say, my first non-move!

DON'T BE AFRAID TO GAMBLE

Look around and see if you can exit the situation without bumping him, and counter him by making a move of your own. Use the landscape to conceal your movement, then come at him from a different angle, a little closer. This represents to him that a hen has moved or that a new hen has come in. Often just a simple cluck or two will be all it takes. On a different note, remember that belly crawling can also be a good move. There are a lot of people who are avidly against belly crawling, just as there are those who swear by it. Please keep in mind that this is a dangerous move on public land. But if it's just for a few yards, I'll often use it to reposition myself. It's proven to be a successful tactic.

REEVALUATE WHAT YOU'RE DOING IN MID-GAME

Given that you and the turkey are in a stalemate, rethink your hunt in the heat of the moment. (Hey, it's not like you don't have time! Usually you've been sitting there listening to him scream at you for several minutes . . . even hours!) Ask yourself, "Am I doing anything wrong? Am I out of position? Is there a barrier between us, like a creek, fence, shelf, or ridge?" By using the process of elimination, you can often rethink yourself into success.

DON'T OBSESS OVER THE SITUATION

The fate of the universe doesn't hang in the balance of whether or not you tag this tom. Relax. Learn from what he's doing. Let him teach you some new ideas about turkey behavior. There's so much value in doing this – learning from him, trying to see why he's acting a certain way. He'll most likely be there tomorrow. You'll know where to be, too!

FIGHT IF YOU HAVE TO

Few people can avoid watching a real fistfight, and turkeys are no different. Gobblers and hens alike will come investigate a good rumble. Learning to use fighting purrs is a super tactic when working a hung-up gobbler, especially when he has hens with him. I've used this tactic a lot to call the hens and challenge their dominance. The gobbler will often come in tow, and walk right into your gun.

FAKE AN EXIT

If you have a partner, one of you drop back and imitate a hen leaving the area. Just getting him to come that extra thirty yards can be the difference between success and failure. If you don't have a buddy – and if you can do it without giving yourself away – walk back forty yards and call softly. It's the same effect.

COME BACK LATER

Just let him go. I've used this tactic quite a bit. Toms will often revisit a spot later in the day. So give it an hour or so, then return. Or just discipline yourself to shut up for a long while. Let him come snooping around the area again. In the mean-time you can move up closer to where he was, letting him come back to you.

CHAPTER EIGHT

FISHING IN FOUL WEATHER

KNOWING WHEN <u>NOT</u> TO FLIRT WITH DANGER

Fishing a stream in the early minutes of sunup can do something to the soul that no massage therapist could do in two hours. For me—a guy who loves to fly-fish—getting chest deep in a cool running stream with the fog rising up, the water trickling over the small rocks, and just the slight possibility that I might hook a rainbow is very close to my idea of heaven on earth.

I frequent this stream near where I grew up, and occasionally after a huge rain the water will be up and moving quite rapidly. One summer day I decided to strap on my waders, grab my fly rod, and go see what was happening down at one of my holes.

Usually the water is very clear, moving decently, and set up perfectly for trout. When I got near the stream on this day, however, I didn't have to look close to see the change. The water was up—I mean, really up! No more of this clear stream stuff, but that good ol' clay color.

As I stood there on the bank, I came to the realization that my hopes of fishing were just about slim and none.

But how could I justify leaving on such a pretty day, huh? So in typical fashion for me, I began to contemplate even a remote strategy. I'd feel cheated if I didn't at least *try* to fish!

I'D FEEL CHEATED IF I DIDN'T AT LEAST TRY TO FISH!

WORKING A PLAN

I made my way down a field, closer to a spot where I knew it was usually very shallow. The river is wide there, so naturally I figured it wouldn't be too bad. I was guessing that even with the water up, it would probably be just around my mid-waist and at least fishable.

In getting there I had my assumptions confirmed—and then some! Yes, it was mid-waist, but moving much quicker than I thought. I stood there for about ten minutes, just watching the water move, debating whether I should go in or go home.

I decided to inch my way out, ever so slowly, dragging my feet to keep from losing contact with solid ground. I had made it only five feet from where I had started when I realized that the water was moving much too fast, and I needed to abort mission . . . *right then!*

THE WHOLE THING WAS BIGGER THAN I WAS.

Now came the challenge: walking back upstream to my origin, because by now, downstream was much too deep. I struggled, but made it back to the water's edge. In all honesty, though, I was a little shaken. I never should have attempted to fish. The elements were much too dangerous. The current was too strong, my environment was not completely familiar to me, and I was alone. The whole thing was bigger than I was, and I really could have ended up being hurt or even drowned.

ABANDONING SHIP

Often in life, we find ourselves messing around in uncharted waters.

Sometimes it's temptation—the currents of emotion are moving much too strongly for our safety. Sometimes it's pride—the fact that we all tend to believe we're bigger and stronger than we really are. Unfortunately, this can land us in places where we find ourselves alone and not as capable as we once thought.

On the stream that day, I just didn't use my head. Yes, I may have been able to fish for a few minutes—only to have a submerged log, rolling like thunder from the force of the current, clip my feet and take me under. Would those few minutes of fishing pleasure have been worth injury or death?

Yet we do the same thing in life, don't we?

People risk a lifetime of investment for a few minutes of pleasure.

People risk a lifetime of investment for a few minutes of pleasure. They may throw away years of marriage for a temporary fling. They may embezzle a few thousand dollars from their company over several years, only to be fired and lose hundreds of thousands of dollars in potential salary that would have been theirs over the long haul.

God gave us His Holy Spirit to be not only a Comforter but a Counselor, too. Maybe today—or sometime next week—you'll come upon a stream of life where you'll feel a magnetic pull to fish it out. Remember: play it safe and don't wade in. Most likely it really is bigger and stronger than you are, and the consequences can be potentially fatal. Get God's counsel on the situation and use it.

No temptation has overtaken you except what is common to humanity. God is faithful and He will not allow you to be tempted beyond what you are able, but with the temptation He will also provide a way of escape, so that you are able to bear it.

DEAD DRIFTING DOWNSTREAM

GOING AGAINST CONVENTIONAL WISDOM CAN BE SUCCESSFUL

In addition to the usual fly-fishing method, I've employed a non-traditional approach for fly presentation with great success. One of my favorite streams is somewhat lazy when it comes to current. The water gently moves along. And when I've tried to fish upstream there in a traditional manner, I often can't feel the strike because my line holds so much slack and is somewhat lifeless. That's why I've started using a variation of "dead drifting" when I fish there. Traditional dead drifting involves standing parallel with the stream – your back to the shore – and casting upstream while letting your fly drift to the fish. Using a bit of a non-traditional approach, however, I move *above* the fish, let out a lot of line, and allow my fly to present itself downstream from my position. The submerged fly looks very natural. It just moves along in the lazy current, right to the fish's location. This ends up giving me much more control and a quicker read on a good bite.

MEND YOUR LINE

Because you're letting out a lot of line, it can straighten out quickly and move your fly faster than the current is moving. Since this appears abnormal to a fish, it can cause him to pass up your fly. So keep your line "mended" – that is, keep it resembling lazy "s" patterns in the water. Slow it down and make things look natural.

STAY LOW

Because you are upstream from a fish when you're dead drifting, you can easily be spotted. So one of the keys I've found in using this method with success is *staying low.* It's normally best to move quite a ways up from him, fishing from your knees as you crouch in the stream.

BE AWARE OF YOUR LOCATION

This type of fishing won't work in all streams. Mountain streams, for one, won't allow this kind of line length because of the boulders that are present. If you're fishing in really fast water, this too can make it hard to control the speed of your line. But moderate to slow waters can give you some great action when you use this fishing technique. Try it. You might find out that dead drifting has more life than any other tactic you've tried before!

STILL, NOTHING WRONG WITH THE OLD TRIED-AND-TRUE

Yes, trout normally face upstream. We know that. They sit there and let the current bring their food to them, which is only smart – why should they work for their food when the current can be their waiter? So most people who fly-fish like to cast upstream, above a trout's nose, and present their fly in a traditional fly-fishing manner. It's a classic technique, because it keeps your body behind the fish so you avoid spooking him.

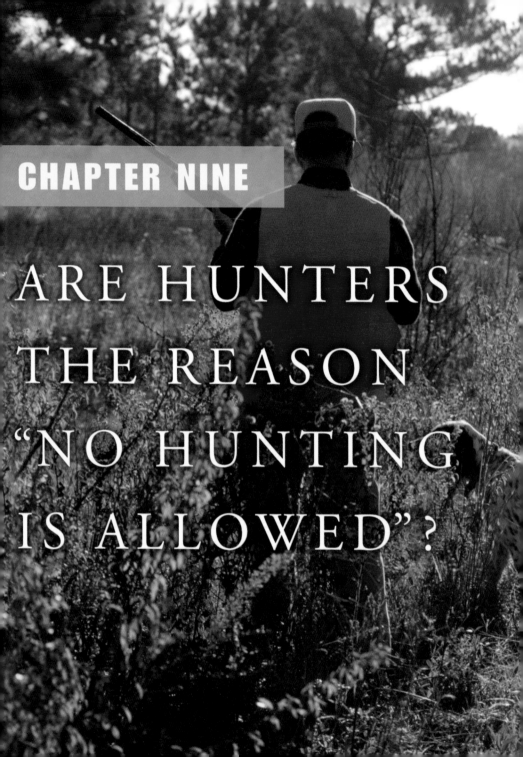

CHAPTER NINE

ARE HUNTERS THE REASON "NO HUNTING IS ALLOWED"?

I f you've been around the sport of hunting for very long, then you know this: access to land can be precious and priceless. It wasn't always this way, of course. When I started hunting as a young boy, leasing land to hunt on was a totally foreign concept. Today, it's just the opposite. Enjoying land you can hunt on without having to pay for it is a rare gift.

Perhaps like me, you've been blessed over the years with access to various farms around your home turf. But because (as it sometimes plays out) farms change ownership or unexpected events pop up, you know how easily you can lose these privileges and be left "hunting" for hunting land!

Recently some of this bad fortune fell into my life and sent me reeling for places to exercise my passion for the outdoors.

HUNTING LAND

As you can imagine, I was in a panic. Gobbler days were staring at me fast and hard, and I was running out of time. So I hopped in my truck and started driving the back roads, stopping at farms and talking to landowners. And although many of them said they simply couldn't allow any hunting on their place, I did manage to pick up a farm or two, which was good. I now had access to some new dirt—just in time for turkey season.

But I have to admit I was bothered by a common response I heard from landowners—a response that hit heavily on my heart.

Time after time, different landowners told me there was one reason why they had stopped allowing hunting on their property: the hunters them-selves. Farmer after farmer told me, "I let this fellow hunt, and before I knew it, there was litter all over my place."

Time after time, different landowners told me there was one reason why they had stopped allowing hunting on their property: the hunters themselves.

ALL A MAN'S WAYS SEEM RIGHT IN HIS OWN EYES, BUT THE LORD WEIGHS THE MOTIVES.

PROVERBS 16:2

One older landowner said, "I told this one ol' boy he could hunt. But one day as I drove down to the farm to pick up something from the barn, there were three trucks down there: his and two others from two different counties! I had told one man he could hunt, and instead he had brought all his friends down to hunt with him."

Another farmer—one of the few who still makes his sole living at it—added to my disgust when he told me how a certain man was hunting both his place *and* the adjacent property without asking the neighbor's permission. Get this—the abusive hunter had even torn down some of the barbwire fence between the two properties by stepping on it, thus costing the landowner money to repair the fence, not to mention lots of apologies for the damage his cattle had done to his neighbor's land.

From trampling on their good nature to trespassing on their property, too many hunters are getting landowners fed up with hunting altogether!

GROUND RULES

If your state requires you to have a Hunter's Safety Education Certificate to be able to hunt legally, then I must ask you this question: "What were some of the first rules you learned?"

(1) Treat every gun as if it were loaded until you check it yourself.

(2) Leave a landowner's property exactly the way you found it.

My hunter's safety teacher drilled these concepts into my little brain so I'd never forget them, and I carry these truths with me even to this day. So I guess I was fairly surprised that day when I was out on the roads searching for new land to hunt—surprised that I'd have to spend an equal amount of time apologizing for the mistakes of the hunting community at large.

The bottom line is this: landowners (as well as the general public) form opinions of hunters based on how you and I act. The landowners I dealt with that day had very deep opinions (mostly negative) about hunters, even though their opinions were primarily based on a handful of experiences with a small segment of the hunting population.

The bottom line is this: landowners (as well as the general public) form opinions of hunters based on how you and I act.

So for the sake of hunting and hunters everywhere, remember one of the golden rules of the outdoors: "Leave a landowner's property exactly the way you found it."

This is a simple matter of integrity and class.

Just think it through: Your good name is far more important than any trophy animal you bag while you're out breaking the rules or simply being disrespectful. Taking advantage of a landowner is an issue of poor character. It gives hunting a bad reputation.

Remember, it may not be fair, but the people you encounter in life think of *you* when they think of hunting. Be sure you carry the titles of "hunter" and "outdoorsman" with dignity!

A GOOD NAME IS MORE DESIRABLE THAN GREAT RICHES; TO BE ESTEEMED IS BETTER THAN SILVER OR GOLD.

—PROVERBS 22:1

"A peculiar virtue in wildlife ethics is that the hunter ordinarily has no gallery to applaud or disapprove of his conduct. Whatever his acts, they are dictated by his own conscience, rather than by a mob of onlookers. It is difficult to exaggerate the importance of this fact."

—Aldo Leopold

WINNING A LAND-OWNER'S HEART

KEY 1: LEAVE A LANDOWNER'S PROPERTY EXACTLY THE WAY YOU FOUND IT

The most frequent complaint heard from landowners who shut down hunting on their farms is that their property was being abused or mistreated. Many hunters treat God's great outdoors as if it were a trash can. Nothing can cost you your hunting privileges faster than littering property. But more than just litter, remember that landowners have things set up a certain way on their farm for a reason. If you find a gate open, leave it open. If you open a gate, close it as soon as you go through it – not after you've finished hunting. Many a hunter has lost privileges from leaving a gate open, sending the farmer chasing down his cattle and having to repair damage to his neighbor's property.

KEY 2: BE SURE YOU ARE FULLY AWARE OF THE LANDOWNER'S EXPECTATIONS, AND ABIDE BY THEM

If a landowner gives you permission to hunt, that doesn't mean he gave your buddies permission, too! If you want to bring other people with you, never assume the landowner is open to it. Ask him! Most of the time he won't mind. But often he will. Just cover your bases. And if the landowner wants you to call first before coming, then never just show up. Respect his wishes. The alternative is that you may lose your privileges altogether. Just do what they say, and you'll be fine.

KEY 3: PERMISSION TO HUNT ONE PERSON'S PROPERTY IS NOT AN INVITATION TO HUNT THE NEIGHBOR'S

Trespassing is illegal! Plus, it can cause major problems between the landowner and the people who live around him. The only thing it may cost *you* are your hunting privileges, but the landowner still has to live there with an angry neighbor when you're gone.

KEY 4: OFFER TO HELP WITH UPKEEP OF THEIR PROPERTY

Many landowners are farmers, and a farmer's work is never done! On top of that, all landowners have property taxes. The bottom line is: owning land isn't cheap. So if he's willing to let you hunt on his place, offer to help him bale hay, bush hog, clean out fence rows, paint the barn, or just be available. Make it very clear that you really do want to help the landowner and try to repay him for his kindness.

KEY 5: SEND OCCASIONAL GIFTS

Nothing can warm a farmer's heart like a $50 gift certificate to a farm supply center, the co-op, or the local hardware store. Send him a dinner for two at a local restaurant, or send a gift basket on a holiday. Just let him know how much you appreciate access to his land. Make him glad he told you "yes."

CHAPTER TEN

TEST

PATTERNING

YOUR HEART

FULL CHOKE OR
IMPROVED CYLINDER?

Picture this: It's two months before opening day. You're literally counting down the time until you can get your feet back in the field once again. But it's still two months away. That's sixty grueling days. So what do you do?

Well, if you're anything like me, you want your gear in top shape before you chase your favorite quarry. That's why one of my top priorities during the downtime before hunting season is to be sure my gun or bow is performing at the optimum level.

I begin shooting my bow in the early summer. With my gun, however, I'm not quite as far out. Usually it's at that two-month benchmark when I'll begin patterning my firearms. It seems to take the edge off of cabin fever, and I feel like I'm speeding up the hours until opening day.

SHOOTING OFF

During some recent pre-season shooting, I began to notice inconsistency in my shotgun. It was simply patterning all over the place. I knew I wasn't moving on my shots, given that I was bench shooting off of sandbags.

No, something was definitely wrong.

For lack of a better term, I was noticing patterns within patterns. Instead of a nice, even displacement of shot when I'd shoot at my target, I'd end up with clusters of shots scattered all around the general target area.

Realizing I had a definite problem, I sent my gun to a ballistics company. They tested it out and confirmed that I did, in fact, have a consistency problem. My shot load was far too distributed—spread too thin—which resulted in a lack of punching power. The ballistics company did some

WE GIVE OURSELVES TO SO MANY DIFFERENT THINGS, OUR LIVES BECOME VIRTUALLY INSIGNIFICANT IN THE LONG RUN.

custom work to the gun, added a new choking system, and fixed my damaged confidence.

Within a few days of getting my gun back, I was out at the range once again—this time with eager anticipation.

It only took one shot to see the difference! An even distribution of pellets. No clusters or blobs. My target area was saturated with a high concentration of shot, thus bringing back the punch I needed in order to take game with one shot.

In short, what the ballistics company had done was take a scattered gun which was patterning erratically and had concentrated its power toward one central point.

CONCENTRATED EFFORT

There's an important life lesson here if you really think about it.

We no longer live in the fast lane; we live at warp speed. And as far as I know, they haven't even created a lane for that yet! But given our hectic lifestyles, we end up spreading ourselves way too thin. The result is a life of little spiritual substance. No depth.

It has been said that many people are a mile wide and an inch deep. We give ourselves to so many different things, our lives become virtually insignificant in the long run. Much of what we invest in seems urgent, yet often these same things prove to be of little importance. God becomes just another pellet on a paper target filled with holes . . . one among many.

How much better if we were an inch wide and a mile deep!

How different would you be right now if you were living with a concentrated purpose?

What would your world look like if you led a life of highly concentrated, focused energy—focused on all the right things instead of giving your attention to anything and everything?

Today, if you were to take an honest assessment, what would the shot pattern of your life look like on paper? When it comes to what you invest in, would you say that your patterns are inconsistent? Is the domain of your heart randomly spread about, or do you have high velocity, focused energy?

Jesus said, "Seek first the kingdom of God and His righteousness, and all these things will be provided for you" (Matthew 6:33).

That, friend, is the definition of concentration—to place the bead of your heart and mind on the one true target.

"Seek first the kingdom of God and His righteousness, and all these things will be provided for you."
—Matthew 6:33

DON'T COLLECT FOR YOURSELVES TREASURES ON EARTH, WHERE MOTH AND RUST DESTROY AND WHERE THIEVES BREAK IN AND STEAL. BUT COLLECT FOR YOURSELVES TREASURES IN HEAVEN, WHERE NEITHER MOTH NOR RUST DESTROYS, AND WHERE THIEVES DON'T BREAK IN AND STEAL. FOR WHERE YOUR TREASURE IS, THERE YOUR HEART WILL BE ALSO.

—MATTHEW 6:19-21

CHAPTER ELEVEN

A CHAPTER ONLY YOU CAN DECIDE TO WRITE

I hope you have been helped throughout this book in your quest for the game you pursue. And I hope I've challenged you to open your heart to the many things the outdoors provides—things which go far beyond guns, camo, and rods and reels.

More than anything, though, I hope I've challenged you to come to a place in your life where you can see beyond this created world and see into the eternal world. No matter how good of an outdoorsman you are, you too will one day reach your final season.

There will be no more opening days.

Life will be over.

What then?

One thing is for sure: if you are an outdoorsman, you are certainly without excuse. Remember Romans 1:20—that God's power and greatness "have been clearly seen, being understood through what He has made"? You have been fully exposed to God by being exposed to the outdoors. But are you strong enough to accept His great love?

When God sent Jesus into our world, He was hunting, too. He had you in His sights. He was bound and determined to seek you out, only to pour His love and hope upon you. All you have to do is receive His love into your heart for it to come alive and transform you.

You'll never have all your questions answered on this side of heaven. What you *can* have, however, is hope beyond your imagination, power beyond your personal strength, and peace which you cannot find through any product on the market.

It all comes through a trusting relationship with Jesus.

The choice is yours, and only you can choose to connect with God through a relationship with Jesus Christ. When it comes to this specific issue, only you can decide what happens in the storyline of your life.

It's the most important chapter of your life story that you'll ever write.

I hope you'll really think seriously about this. I'm praying that we'll not only have our love for the outdoors in common. I'm praying that we'll have Jesus in common, too.

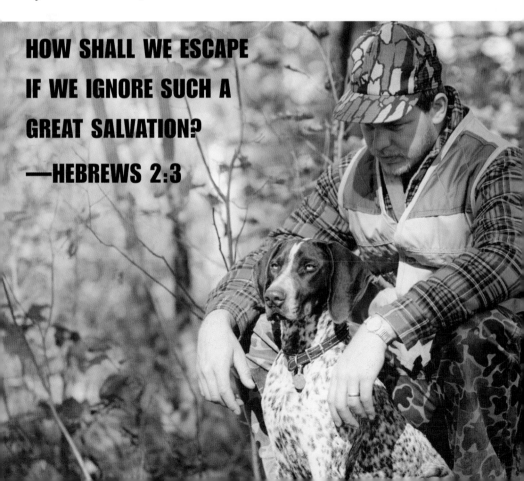

HOW SHALL WE ESCAPE
IF WE IGNORE SUCH A
GREAT SALVATION?
—HEBREWS 2:3

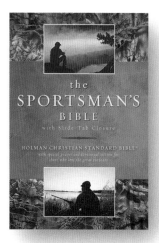

Now Available!

THE SPORTSMAN'S BIBLE

Featuring:

- "Superflauge® Game" camo-cover with slide-tab
- Devotions for hunters and fishermen
- Tips, code of conduct, and safety info
- Topical guide to specific Bible passages
- Largest typesize of any pocket Bible available
- Holman Christian Standard Bible text
- Gift boxed, non-glare pages, and more

Retail Value $29.99

Value Price $19.97

ISBN: 1-58640-095-9

Available wherever books and Bibles are sold.